LOOSE SHEETS

Alessio Zanelli

UPFRONT PUBLISHING
LEICESTERSHIRE

LOOSE SHEETS
Copyright © Alessio Zanelli 2000

All Rights Reserved

ISBN 1 84426 025 9

First Published 2000 by
MINERVA PRESS

Second Edition 2002 by
UPFRONT PUBLISHING
Leicestershire

LOOSE SHEETS

*To those making a blanket for night-cold
out of fleeting moments of happiness*

He who desires but acts not, breeds pestilence.

William Blake

About the author

Alessio Zanelli was born on 12 February 1963 in Cremona, a small, quiet town not far from Milan, on the left bank of the river Po, in northern Italy, renowned for its makers of stringed instruments (especially the violin makers of the past, such as Antonio Stradivari).

He attended the Scientific Lycée 'Aselli' and then attempted to go to university, but for many reasons he never completed his electronics engineering studies. Since 1991 he has been working for a bank and at the moment is concerned with the advice to customers about their investments.

He has been studying English since the early eighties and began writing poetry in 1985, at first also in Italian and afterwards exclusively in English. What spurred him on to learn a completely new language (at High School he had studied German) was the need to understand the lyrics of songs by pop-rock bands such as Pink Floyd, Emerson Lake & Palmer and Deep Purple, his first musical loves. Later, fascinated by the richness and malleability of the language, he started reading American and British literature, with a particular predilection for poetry. So he read – in their mother tongue – Whitman, Melville, Masters, Poe, Dickinson, Blake, Yeats, Keats, Eliot and Thomas among others. Over fifteen years, he has written more than two hundred poems, the best of which are gathered together to form *Loose Sheets*, his very first publication.

Love, as it almost always happens to poets, is the main theme, but much of the verse is inspired by the various aspects of nature, of human mind and of men's vicissitudes through time and history.

When he is not working – besides studying English usage and literature and writing poetry – he devotes himself to reading ancient history, science fiction and modern physics, and to listening to music. He also loves to travel, having visited the UK and the USA several times, paint and spend time away with old friends. They once formed a large company of unbridled madmen (see the poem 'The King Of The Fax', dedicated to the head of such a crazy troop), now reduced to a small group made of those who have survived the conventionality and restrictions due to work-career, marriage and social attitudes.

Contents

Part II

Soulbeads

Part III

Loose Sheets

Part IV

A Lunatic's Sentences

Part V

Back To The Cradle Gaol

Part VI

Accidental Verse

That Summer

Free Yourself

Listen to the wind hiss
And feel its sweet kiss –

Here to caress you,
Not to alarm you.

Let down your hair,
Yielding is so fair;

Unleash your weary mind,
The unexpected you will find.

Unchain your fantasy,
Indulge in ecstasy –

The breeze is just waiting,
Free yourself breathing.

12 July 1985

Power Of Sleep

Now you really have a reason not to sleep –
Of being the Devil I have been dreaming deep.

13 July 1985

Slapstick Guys

We alone are the guys,
We alone are the bankers –
To monopolize attention,
To draw the eyes of all.
We alone play with girls,
We intimidate anybody –
To root boredom out,
To show all our nothingness.
We alone are the guys –
We're nothing but a troop of imbeciles.

14 July 1985

No Poetry

Twittering of birds
As delight of a moment;
Magic sound of words
In close love enjoyment.

Sweet-acrid scent of fields
And charming maiden's tress;
Shadowy quiet of wealds
And loving woman's caress.

All things which someone tore,
All things I don't know anymore.

15 July 1985

God's Plan Escaped

What I am nobody can say,
Neither you nor God, nay, nay;
I have escaped His control
To be something really foul.

16 July 1985

Cry Of A Child

Don't cry
Sweet scared creature;
No lie
I can say about the future.

Don't cry
Little innocent child;
I'll try
Unto you to be mild.

Don't ask
The reason of all that;
No mask,
I know you're upset thereat.

Don't ask
Why the world is so evil;
No mask,
Seeing everywhere upheaval.

But do take now what's given you,
One day you'll be grown-up too.
You could try to change this world
Where men no longer fear the Lord,
But only swing the hatred sword.

17 July 1985

Creature Of Cold

I am a creature of cold,
Nothing warm was I ever told –

I love the expanses of snow,
Give me ice right here and now.

I cannot suffer the hot air,
Being an icy crystal is so fair.

I am a creature of cold,
I can be glacial and yet bold –

Can you then tell me ready
Why there's fire inside my body?

I am a creature of cold,
Nothing warm was I ever told.

17 July 1985

In The Middle

All my winding way along
In the middle I've kept strong.
This is the mocking result:
I have never lost,
I have never won.

17 July 1985

Every Moment Thou Livest

Beautiful,
An angel thou art
When thou keepest silent
In a thought corner of thine,
And absorb'd,
Prying into thy morrow.

Beautiful,
With glamor thou shinest
When thou freshly sheddest
Thy sweet unfathomable smile
All around thee,
And thy face mastereth me.

Beautiful,
Love thou art
When thou warily rollest,
Just only licking my gaze,
Thy wondrous eyes,
And courageously wishest to look into my mind.

Day after day lovely and lovely
In every gesture thou makest,
In every word thou sayst,
In every expression thou hast,
Most beauteous thou art,
In every moment thou livest.

20 July 1985

Like A Comet Falls

Like a comet falls
In boundless spaces,
An entire stranger
To the surrounding universe,
And forever and ever
Streaks the blue of the sky –
So I've fallen in love.
Deep in estranging love.

20 July 1985

The Watcher

Not a mere observer,
Not a common man,
He never can be seen,
But his existence is sure.
From some planet up there,
From some unknown sat
He can look at all minutely –
Nothing can escape him.
His eyes see the sky,
His eyes see all men,
He is not a God at all,
But only watches the universe.
His pain lasts forever,
In solitude forever;
He can never interfere,
Nothing he can alter.
This is his condemnation,
This his perpetual task –
Observer of men's history,
Watcher of the world.

24 July 1985

What Hath Thy Son Become, Mother?

Lots of worries afflicting,
A thousand questions persisting,
Never-ending unmerited trouble:
Where dost thou take this force, mother?

25 July 1985

Slowly

Slowly, slowly,
Maybe there is a way;
Slowly, slowly,
Don't be ahead
Of your times.
I beg you,
I implore you,
We can't turn back,
But we can begin again.
Slowly, slowly,
Maybe there is a way.

25 July 1985

Cut Off By Atropos

Jupiter alone
Maybe could know
What upon me
The Three Fates decided.
But I don't want
Any God to show me my future;
Her duty Atropos
Has already done well.

Undated

Burned Fields (That Summer)

That summer,
Those few days of sun,
They burned the arid fields.
And with them,
Me.

24 November 1985

Winterhope

Shut up myself in my own stronghold,
Sheltered from the new winter's chill,
As the hearth of some soul dries my ancient tears –
Alive – the all-burning blaze reinflames,
Alive – the past days' hope returns.
They both and they alone –
Two tyrants chasing me like shadows,
Two that will never die.

24 November 1985

Soulbeads

Won't This Winter End?

How difficult it is
To find some inspiration
Now that the summer tempest is gone,
With its stunning thunders
And transfixing bolts.
How sadly onerous it is
To find true happy words
Now that a mute gray sky
Of the upsetting storm
Has taken the place.
But terrible and full with vigor
Still wanders 'round the storm
With impetuous threatening winds,
Over this gloomy sky
Which hides some ancient pain.
Let it cease, this flat winter!
Let them cease, these lifeless days!
The storm will return to rage,
For my heart – in the eye of the cyclone –
Knows that after the tempest only
The sun can shine.

30 November 1985

Waiting For The Snow

Misted panes
Let come to me
A dimmed vision
Of the world outside.
Through that window
In my faithful room
The same scene always,
Every day one only picture.
Colors,
They don't change either
In that immovable
Weary view outside there.
Winter being almost here,
I should cry even more
As everyone thinks
Of the forthcoming new spring.
And behind misted panes
Only I lonely remain,
Waiting for the snow
With its bright mantle.
And for my soul to clear.

3 December 1985

36

Forgotten Prince

There once was a lone prince,
He was bold and also strong;
No one's seen him long since,
He's disappeared all along.

Someone says he still lives
In some place out of sight;
Only solitude he conceives,
And keeps on sitting tight.

Someone else tells other tales:
He would reign over a barren land
Haunted only by the fury of gales,
Over a stretch of rock and sand.

Yet for most people he's dead and gone,
This is the truth that fills the air;
No hidden land, no solitude throne,
His old home's now cold and bare.

4 December 1985

Little Blade On A Stony Hill

As thin as baby's breath
I saw a blade of grass,
Struggling unto death,
Stifled by a stone mass.
It had a heroic will,
They didn't let it pass,
Yet they couldn't still
Such a strong yearning;
No stone, no wind, no chill
Could hinder its leaning.
It was only a little blade,
But as long as God willing
Never will come time to fade.

6 December 1985

38

Our Hour

Let us sing, O Muse,
Some last verses –
No more we may abuse
Our spirit's senses.
Too long the songs we've sung
Imbued have the air –
Over us God's wrath hung
And we did not care.
As winds were silent
For hearing Thee,
We deem'd it the moment
To set our essence free.
We thought we were born again
Elevating Thy chant,
Yet we were deep in pain,
For we needed Thy grant.
Now Thou alone, O Muse,
Canst beg forgiveness
For our impious misuse
And for our unfaithfulness.
Let us sing a prayer,
For we have gone sour –
To quieten is so fair,
Let us now wait for our hour.

10–11 December 1985

The Girl Who Saw An Angel

I don't remember when,
But well I know what
Magic words yours were –
They really struck me a lot.
Maybe it was an evening
Before less happy nights,
We two alone were speaking,
Sitting by dim mystic lights.
You were so transported,
Telling your singular tale,
I was lovingly enchanted –
You made me nearly quail.
Truth told your soft lips,
Your simplicity was sincere –
You didn't say any quips
And took me into a magic sphere.
I little know who you are,
I suspect you to be an angel,
Yet you said you only are
The girl who saw an angel.

12 December 1985

Abandoned Swing

Do you remember
That night of June,
The starry sky,
The light breeze,
That silence
All around us?
Time truly seemed
To stop for us
And I, bewitched,
Near you standing,
Could hear your heartbeat
Throbbing within your breast.
It was all so quiet
But our hearts,
Your eyes twinkled
By the light of stars;
My words alone
There were, and yours.
Do you remember
In that court of ours
The twilight charm,
The moonlight shadow,
The swing
You were sitting on?
We've gone back there
Nevermore together,
And now that swing,
With all its secrets,
In the court keeps silent,
And no echo can slip it.

A point in time is there,
Whereto my past, my present,
My future, my life flow.
The abandoned swing is the keeper
Of what in the aftertime came,
But that is another tale.

12 December 1985

Come Lyin' Down, O Icy Rime

Come lyin' down, O icy rime,
And make these pale grasses
With your crystal whiteness shine.
This clear sky invites you
To softly cover each spot of ground.
As long as the night lasts
Extend your fine freezing veil
On the blades, on the leaves,
On the quiet stretches of water,
On every silent corner of land.
The dawn will give you the light
That you may start to sparkle
To the cold winter morning sky.
Thence this clear starry night
Belongs to you and your lively white.
Thence this night – just once again –
Come lyin' down, O icy rime.

14 December 1985

43

Leaves Fall And The Swallow Leaves

Summer's gone
To the southern hemisphere,
And tardy sunsets
Don't paint anymore
West horizons purple.
Every year – for a long time –
Someone silently cries
When
Leaves fall and the swallow leaves.

15 December 1985

I Mourn You, Placid Prairies

I mourn you, placid prairies
I once ran carefree through,
I pine for you, sweet smelling fields
Where – as an unaware child –
I us'd to hide myself.
Where are you, serene days of childhood?
And you, clear skies of distant summer ev'nings?
I have lost you, places of a timeless happiness,
And you, theatres of my first intact emotions.
Then life flow'd like the lines
Of an unknown song,
And there was place for gladness
In rainy days too; then I relish'd
The trembling wait for tomorrow, and love
Was nothing but a remote word.
Where are you, my missing friends of that time?
And you, old village-men with your ancient tales?
I have not forgotten you, nor my infancy seasons,
But it's all so buried under the weight
Of my own present.
I weep over you, distant sunny lands,
How much water they have pour'd – your rivulets,
I yearn for you, sorrowless days of the past,
Cherish memories clear,
And cherish some of me.

18 December 1985

Before That Night Comes

Impalpable, a snowdust
Pauses in the air,
Reminding hearts in anxiety
Of the coming of a Holy Night.
Imperceptible, it spreads
A rare happiness,
Inebriating, an aura
Among the souls of amazed men.
It won't be the same Christmas
To each heart that lives,
It won't be the same peace night
To each soul that hopes.
And so, even though by then
I won't be close to you,
Remember my love,
Before that night comes.

23 December 1985

Photographing Sunday

'Twas last Sunday afternoon,
And the sun enlarg'd upon the blinding snow;
Anguish could have o'ertaken me very soon,
Thence I made for a nature show.
I would seize images of serenity,
As happy children on their sledges,
But I shot my solitude captivity,
And your face shining through the edges.

15 January 1986

The Revenge Of The Pierced Man

Growing in the air
Is the yell of rage
The poor pierced man
Wholly feeds on the spirit
Of his old wounds.
But it's not delirium
Through thirst for revenge
Which is issuing now
From his revolted being.
It's not any vengeance
Such a poor man can desire,
Or even only conceive.
And yet some vengeance
Can be expected and feared,
So that the Undiscernible Cause
Will lose all its conquests.
But who are you,
Undiscernible Cause,
Named doom by men,
That can wish nothing
And pursue no aim
But determine all?
That does not matter
To the pierced man,
For he has no reason
Nor any why to get to.
And he can't be a fool
For not wanting to know,
For not seeking redemption
And for his squeals of pain.

He's not seeking vengeance
For there's nothing defined
To ascribe the ills to.
And yet there'll be a vengeance –
Some anonymous one;
And you, eyeless doom,
And Undiscernible Cause,
Shan't shatter lives anymore,
Shan't open wounds anymore.
It'll be like bending you to us,
You that always bend us to you!
It'll be the revenge of the pierced man –
Once he – unaware of his fate
And thence careless of you –
Has forgotten his past
And defeated his grief.

24 April 1986

I Was Born In The Wrong Place

When suddenly summer
Sweeps away the new spring
And a high burning sun,
Through sultry air filtered,
Of a resurrected nature
The bright green stains,
It is as though that happen'd in me,
As though that sultriness
Crept and spread inside me.
Then, when I see that life bloom
Getting burnt in the haste of time,
And my soul – just born again –
Becoming arid in few intense days,
Like the fields beneath the sun,
Then I feel
I was born in the wrong place.

Always, when someone taps
On my door set ajar
And I don't care to answer,
My mind is somewhere else
To run after distant dreams,
Far away from this torrid moor
And over some freezing expanse,
Where nothing gets ruin'd
By the flames of an instant.
Then, when I lock my door
And untie the wings of my mind
To fly over fantastical realms,
When I run after a never-won love

And don't hear the voices calling me back,
Then I realize
I was born in the wrong place.

4 June 1986

O Hawy

O Hawy,
Can you remember
When I gave you that name?
It was only a joke
You didn't like very much.
We were only shammers
Not knowing our roles.
You were still a child,
But the woman advanced;
I was not a man yet
And wished to be a child.
I will always remember
Your wavering and your blushing
In those magic moments
You were becoming a woman.
I will never forget
Those vehement feelings
You began artlessly
To stir up in me;
Your sweetly cool face,
You heartbreaker,
You at thirteen,
Simply you,
O Hawy.

5 June 1986

To Eva

Now that it's all past
And thou breathest no more,
Now only, I can remember thee.
One cannot be silent or remain unmoved
At the call of blood.
Thy slightly face,
Diaphanous and shaded,
I only remember,
O Eva;
But great is the feeling,
And sadly wordless,
That joineth me unto thee.
Cruel fate is thine
Which plac'd death
Upon thy way,
To wait for thee
In the prime of youth.
It wanted to catch thy life
And thou couldst not choose.
Unceasing rains
On a gloomy day
In the heart of June
Were the presage
Of thy premature passing away.
Not tears, nor mourning for thee,
Who maybe hast not even been
Able to weep thy fortunes.
Life bereav'd thee
Of many affections,
Dispensing griefs
And grudge around thee.

In spite of all that
Thou wert running
On the path of happiness,
But thy lot didn't spare unto thee
The only hug thou didst not need,
That icy one of death.
Thou, who from yonder
Clearly seest everything,
Thou maybe know'st,
O Eva,
This is not any farewell,
This is my 'see thee soon'.

12 June 1986

The Black

Where's my throne? Can't see it at all.
Where's my castle? Can't see it at all.
Where's my realm? Can't see it at all.
Where's my soul? Can't see it at all.
Where's my blood? Can't see it at all.
Where's my love? Can't see it at all.
There's the Black! Can see it alone.

11 December 1986

Bells

Near the hamlet,
In every corner, ancient or new,
Or far, far in the foggy country,
Or farther, in the shining sun,
All can hear your message
When you sadly spread
Your old tolling, a dull metal cry,
All around the village.
Those tolls, as chilly blades,
Reach into our hearts and rip out a bit
Of our secret common soul.
Because when we hear that sound,
Unmistakable, everywhere,
From the steeple on the little hill,
We know a piece of us has gone,
Someone has left us forever.

11 December 1986

Loose Sheets

The Knight Errant Of Sorrowland

Tell me – good Knight –
Which is my adventure?
The one of the Questing Beast
Or the one of the Black Shield?
Tell me – noble Sir –
Where can I find fame and glory?
Perhaps in the Perilous Forest
Or inside the Maids' Castle?
No, there's no adventure for me!
Too high were the virtues
Of the Round Table Knights
So that I may be as valiant.
But no champion nor king –
Be he Tristram or Lancelot,
Be he Gawain or Galahad himself –
Could excel me in my joust.
I have no Sangraal to conquer,
No fair damsel to set free,
But no Knight of any age
Is my equal in subduing sorrow.

27 July 1988

The Pantomime Of The Hunter Without Prey

What a clever, unaware actor
Is he, the miserable hunter,
With his spotted pointer
And the leveled shotgun!
Even the dog plays a part:
Smelling, scratching, baying,
Running hither and thither,
Like chasing an inexistent prey.
And he, skilful and silent
To follow the panting poor beastie,
Slave to his perfect insanity.
It's the pantomime
Of the hunter without prey,
Who wanders through the woods,
Untiringly,
With his spotted dog,
Faithful to his resigned lunacy.
For he can't know at all
He's only an actor,
And his dog will never set,
And his gun will never fire.
For there's no prey to hunt,
No victim but himself.

22 August 1988

The Black Stone Of The Sky

Look, you with a swerved mind,
At the Black Stone of the sky,
Look, you unaware and blind,
And be not fool'd by your eye.
Do forget the slothful deities
That crept out from ignorance,
Dispel the ancient frailties
Camouflaged with arrogance!
Turn out the shining stars
Twinkling in their agony,
Cease the celestial wars
Fomented by dark cosmogony.
Stop, and behold, you shy,
Look at it in all its might –
The Black Stone of the sky,
Far brighter than any light.
That's all you must admire,
The silent arcane icy stone
Upon the summit of the spire;
Steady in space, in time alone,
From nothing's edge it fell,
And set the universe all around,
And bore Heaven and Hell,
And Earth, from sky to ground.
Thus, clear your minds and try,
You – slaves to void credences –
To scan the depth of the sky,
But beware of world's appearances.

24 August 1988

Stop The Rotation Of The Earth

Stop the rotation of the Earth
With America under the sun.
Let Europe's glaciers grow
And the air of the continent chill,
That clouds shall prostrate freeze
Over the shapes of the land
Wrapped up in a noiseless dark.
The unbroken shade of the hemisphere
Shall abate the unquiet waters of the seas;
Little by little, the quivers of the soul
Shall deaden, subsiding into
A soundless, lightless quiescence.
Stop the rotation of the Earth
And they will cease – the upsetting whirlpools
Of the mind gripped in the vice
Of inextricable gyres.
Let the world's gears age
In the dust of the arrested time;
Let the brainless, heartless clocks
Keep standstill upon midnight.
Let an unfading sunset
Be immovably reflected
In the middle of the Atlantic,
An imperishable dawn
Spread its gentle dazzle
Athwart the quiet Pacific.
Let it curdle – the blood of men
Dropped from sun-injured wounds;
Let a suave peace
Ascend from my restored body
Up to liberate my mind.

Put an end to the veiled hysteria
Tearing my lax soul, confused
With the ever-changing sky.
Let the Plough be at anchor in the vault
Right above my eyes,
As a beacon to the swaying thought
Bouncing in my brain.
Till from the increased glaciers
A light breeze descends
To refresh the spirit burned
With the alternation of nights and days,
And to blow out
The child-fire of impatience.
Only then the unwarned world
Will begin to turn around again!
But now – please,
If someone exists able to do it –
Stop the rotation of the Earth
With my land in the starlight.

25 August 1988

And The Moon Eclipsed The Sun

Black ravens
O'er hazy hills
Strewn with blood
Of adverse arrays;
Swords shone,
And armors dyed
With brilliant red;
Fury grew as high
As to hurt the sky,
When a chill from the tomb
Struck fervors dumb –
And the moon eclipsed the sun.

Babies cried
Among houses ablaze,
And deaf'ning rumbles
With death inflam'd;
The wind groan'd,
And purple dazzles
Smash'd in the sky;
Blood and destruction
Where'er eyes turn'd,
Then again God Almighty
Griev'd at man's insanity –
And the moon eclipsed the sun.

25 August 1988

The Well

Blood flowers
Ooze ruby tears
On the icy ground

By arcane bowers
Where time's gears
Untiringly round.

The moon cries
Behind faint clouds
Frozen in the breath

Of distant skies
Which bear in crowds
The ghosts of death.

Streams petrify
Into crystal stones,
Whilst fired waves

Blaze and terrify,
And corpses' bones
Writhe in their graves.

Rent sky falls
To cover the ground
As Heaven and Hell

Break middle walls
Of a fictitious bound
To reunite in the Well.

29 August 1988

The Invisible Tie Of Moaning

Eyes see,
And the Heart desires
Joys that hands can't seize;

Joys flee
Like sounds of lyres
Carried by sea breeze.

Those sounds reach
An unknown littoral
Of far-off lands;

There on a beach
Swept by the light Mistral
A lonely Tree stands.

Its boughs
Catch the tunes
Of the distant lyres;

The sea soughs
To the shore dunes
Echoing with far desires.

A Baby cries
On the shore alone,
Scared by the roaring waves;

A wave flies
Up a vale of stone,
Where Old River laves.

Life flows
From Old River's springs
And spreads into the sea;

The sea wind blows,
Strewing from its wings
Life all over the Tree.

Leaves alight
From the Tree on the sand,
Next to the crying Child,

And make him bright
On that desert land,
Drawing life from the wild.

His joy departs,
Flying beyond the sea
Up to the source of moans,

And tells all hearts
Of the River and the Tree,
And of Baby's ceased groans.

30 August 1988

Daydreamer

You see the sun above
Become an angel blue
And fly down to you
Begging for your love.

You see the icy rain
Turn to golden beads
And bless all your deeds
Freeing your soul from pain.

You hear the guns of war
Cease their lethal fires
And strew myriads of flowers
Wreathing many a star.

You lastly hear a voice
Blame your great stupidity,
For while you nurse unreality
True life leaves you no choice.

30 August 1988

To The Unwarlike

Let the gates be open thrown
Of Janus's temple stat'ly,
For unwarlike staying
To idle time away
Suits not your glorious name,
Your power and everlasting fame.

Let vexilla be heighten'd
With imperial eagle grand,
And adorn'd helmets
Do sparkle in the sun,
For if war is ineluctable,
Awaiting is deprecable.

At last let cohorts proud
Be drawn up in legions strong,
And from the Seven Hills
Winds convey to the enemy
Forthcoming army's clamors
Amid history's splendors.

And so you all beware
Of those filthy shadows
That oppress your hearts,
For yielding unto indolence
Will lead you all astray,
And it drove Rome to decay.

31 August 1988

September

September comes,
Clothed in limpid skies
And purple gloamings;
It comes on,
Permeating through the air,
Bringing along
Echoes of distant life
And whispers
Of sedate joy.
September comes,
With fresh breezes
And crystalline nights;
It wraps
Our fidgety souls
In composed euphoria,
Weeping drops of wisdom
To the bottom
Of our trembling hearts.
And sweetly a sigh,
Escaped from angels
Beyond the sky,
Lets us know –
And forget never more –
That summer vanishes
In September days,
While September comes,
And inside us stays.

3 September 1988

All Hallows 1988

Sky's blue changes into violet
To let down the silent sunset;
Mountains below whet their black rim,
Above the hills skylight runs dim.

The winding road drives us crazy
And everything runs vague and hazy;
We've got no eye to see an aim,
But the car flies off all the same.

Minds leave bodies to run away,
But captive souls can't leave the way;
Ground's black joins cool sky's deep blue,
Paints outside a single dark hue.

To each his thoughts, to each his ghost,
We need escape, but we run lost;
We hear a call – some distant thrills –
But we can't go beyond the hills.

2 November 1988

First Time Of The Mind

The Devil is still,
But it stones the heart;
The Angel sings,
But it doesn't ease the pain.
They have got me,
But I have got neither.

The Devil tempts the Angel
And the Angel prompts the Devil
As they dance around my head.
Sin and prayer –
They come as night and day,
But they can't soothe the pain.

Sex kills love
And love kills sex
As the Devil keeps still
And the Angel keeps singing.
The first time of the mind becomes the second,
And the second the third.

Then comes the thousandth one
As the Devil and the Angel smile at each other,
And the false fight empties the spirit.
Love is dead and sex is death
As the mind goes round in dirty circles
And the dream turns to moony stone.

Since I had it –
The first time of the mind,
Since I broke it –
That spell of pureness over her,
Sex is where I seek myself.
Love is where I lost myself.

6 November 1988

Love Age Myths

Ice lances, as hard as steel,
Pierce through your flexible heart,
And hissing in the silence
Like whispers of innocence
You just can but give in to,
They tear your pale soul away.

Once there were the heroes
Who rescued you from woe,
Once there was their power
To force back your shrewd foe.
But time has no scruples
And all myths fade away.

The tyrant proves the torture
As you turn back toward him;
The music dies inside you
Like the twilight in the night.
And love age myths have gone afar –
Gone away like old Tziganes.

11 November 1988

The Fortress

Assault. Desperate assault.
The unmovable walls grew stronger
And my stubbornness went exhausted.
There was no kind of weather
Which could stop my untrimm'd siege,
But there was no kind of assault
Which could break the defense down.
Right as in my childhood games
The Duke led my restless cavalry,
The King of Logris led my arrays,
But God does live in the fortress –
It's never going to fall.
I shot full with my anguish,
I tried with everything I had,
But God permeates the fortress –
It's never going to fall.
John Wayne fired his gun
And King Arthur brandish'd his sword,
But love and war don't live inside there –
Or was it thought it was all a game?
Untiring seasons ran their course
And the rain and the sun follow'd one another
Around the stormproof walls;
The assault ceas'd,
The heroes went back to their graves –
I died to change my lot and make my love alive.
But God does have the fortress –
Therein the Treasure lies untouch'd.

13 November 1988

Roundabout

From the two-sided face,
Elusive and sweet,
Through my eyes,
Enchained forever,
A smooth silhouette,
Ineffaceable, neat,
And the whiteness of the skin,
As rosy as a peach bud,
As cool as a blade –
They entangle my bosom
In an endless rite.
Like a sharp circle
Turns on itself.
Like a deep mystery
Enthralls the mind.

18 November 1988

76

By The Wishin' Well

The unchain'd soul has flown
Like grievance unshown,
Let the body dwell
By the wishin' well.

An old king newborn
Aims the dart unthrown
At all sighs in hell
By the wishin' well.

19 March 1989

Don't Awake The Sleeper

A memory from the future –
Some echo backwards in time,
A warning from the stars
Within inner oneness numberless –
It waves from the silent depths
Of the astral space,
So unfathomable and true,
Master to our anguish,
To the unquiet vacuity of the mind,
Like a remote, arcane menace
Hangs over a frightened child.
Millions of minds
United in the ominous signs
Of the coming unknown,
Issuing from the verge of the universe,
And from the occult abysm of the soul.
Some terrifying prodigy
Feeding on our ancient fear –
The Early Knowledge
Dozing on itself,
Beneath the timeless gaze of God.

30 June 1989

Let The Truth Be Known

I wish to walk
Through the golden gates of beyond
And deep breaths take
In the pure and soft air of wisdom.
I wish to walk
From ev'ry beaten path releas'd
And not forc'd
Into scanty passes
'Twixt obscurely hostile mounts.
Let me get far o'er there –
Sailing before the wind –
O'er of Hercules the pillars stat'ly
So refulgent and murk!
Where the sea it becomes boundless,
Where fear it dies
And the world it's gripp'd in your hand.
I do not wish to await
The ultimate day to rise,
Nor resignedly listen
To the subdued moan of the wind
And the tremendous shriek of the earth.
Then let me search:
For searching is not finding,
Knowing is not realizing!
But these heavy drapes remove
From my icy eyes;
These deaf'ning bells
From my tired ears!
That I may indeed see,
And hear, and lucidly behold,
And for my only fault do wrong.
The world within a hand,

The everlasting dream –
Because a dream it is –
May I fondle it at least,
Of ev'ry futile burden stripp'd,
By the strength alone
Of my newborn mind.
Do not steal them, my dreams,
Truer than anything I see and feel,
Sweeter than true mirth,
Sharper than true pain.
Set it free, Ulysses' spirit:
Out of narrow spaces
Free to rove at last
From time's tyranny releas'd.
Do make possible my peace,
On ev'ryone do bestow their truth,
For there's no greater truth!
A benevolent smile do inspire to Him,
The Lord of Gods,
God to men and all imaginable beings.
Lo! The eagles tireless and unyielding!
Finally clear to them the steepest slopes,
The unchanging peaks
Standing out above perpetual snows,
Up to the sky the high'st ways.
Do not trample
On the tender grass
By the trunks unfruitful and black
Of history's secular trees;
Nor on the unguilty shoots
Growing by the deathless myrtle tree.
Make ev'rything plain to see,
Ev'ry way easy to find,
Before the world it falls down
Collapsing into The One's mind.
Let ev'ryone rise to his throne,
Let the truth be known.

9 July 1989

Throw A Drop Into The Ocean

Throw a drop into the ocean
And it will thank you for this.
You will see the huge expanse of water,
Menacing in its majestic quiet,
Shape smiles unto your eyes
And seethe with unexpected life.
You will hear its endless silence
Turn to tuneful hymns of joy.
Not a bead alone of sweat
Shall be wasted in this vast sea,
Drowsy in an eternal wait.
A minute drop of water
Shall not be lost among the billows,
Powerless in their anger.
You will enrich what's boundless
And gain a safe harbor for the soul.
Throw a drop into the ocean
And – be sure – it will increase.

11 July 1989

Child Soul's Bequest

It hath not faded
The pale glare of the moon
Upon the slated roofs
An' the small steep glaciers
Turn'd to north.
Still the wind it howleth
Along the gurgling stream
An' down the craggy alp.
Still everything
It's in its place:
The aged bridge of wood an' stone,
The grass-grown pastures beneath the crests,
The cozy huts perch'd on the ravines,
The imposing mass of Mount Disgrace.
Everything it keepeth
Its discreet charm,
The shy an' honest pith of yore:
Mountain people's words
As clear as sky's after-storm blue;
Old men's placid stares
As pure as glacial lake water.
Yet it rejoiceth not my spirit –
Alack! Deceiv'd an' restless!
It roameth searching for peace
Up this amiable vale,
Keeper of distant feelings.
But the happy soul,
The thoughtless child soul,
It is yonder petrified,
Yon in the rock –
Its bequest imprisoned

Amidst the eternal ices,
Underneath the unawares
Watchful eye of the eagle.

12 July 1989

To Thee, O Twinkling Star

To thee, O twinkling star,
I do raise my sighs;
To thee, which
From the empyrean vastness
Winkest at my forlorn core,
And before my compliant eyes
Inweavest rays of unearthly peace.
To thee, which
I shall never see nearby,
To thy unkenned refulgence
I do raise
My unheard cries.

13 July 1989

84

A Lunatic's Sentences

The Scream Of The Deep

From beyond the mountains,
From the bottomless deep
Of forgotten casualties
The silent cry emanates.
Human disgraces,
Trampled on and curtained,
Soak the whole earth
And the boundless skies.
As a forsaken child's cry
The echo of centuries evaporates
Amidst the ancient walls,
The dilapidated towers,
The deserted outposts.
In the mute,
Tired, immutable-faced moon
Feats and conquests are mirrored,
And slaughters too.
Blind eyes
Don't see the wonderments of earth,
Yet admire the horrors.
Delighted ears filled with a robin's chirp
Are deaf
To the scream of the deep.

30 July 1989

Invisible Darts

Invisible darts
Shoot through the air,
Heavy and misty,
Laden with unexploded thunders,
Going to disperse
The echoes of far promises
And lighting fires
By the water unquenchable.
The heart it weeps
Because the soft spring snow
By the clear mountain sun
Is swiftly melted:
Thus the illusion,
By insane hopes borne,
Vanishes,
By the mind's whirling won.
And the air
Waxes unbreathable,
So heavy and misty
As to imbue the lungs
With unfathomable woe.
Until a dart again
Reaches the bottom of the heart,
And – whacked, delirious –
In a sobbing groan
The flame goes out.

31 July 1989

The Ant Can Move The Mountain

The sun it shines
To half the world at a time,
The night it quenches
Half the world's thirst at a time.
The full moon it's half the moon –
For eternity a romantic lie!
I could speak to you
For many an hour – hours
Longer than sundown shadows –
Therefore the marvels
Of the simple and the obvious
Make disclosed to your aghast mind.
Still you understand not
The power of the Thought,
Which sooner than the mind
Is a divine appurtenance.
And in speaking of Love,
Like the worst criminal
You just shut it up in a bare cell!
Granting full powers to your mind,
Eternal warder to your fancy for flying!
Meanwhile my Thought it pounces
Upon the fullness of the night;
It satisfies the spirit's
Insatiable thirst for Love.
But the Love I'm speaking of –
Brother to my friend the Thought
And on its untiring wings elevated –
Is not achievable by the mind,
As the highest mountain top
Is not accessible to the tiny ant.

Nevertheless, the ant
It guards the most incredible force,
And knows not Love,
And thence loves not the Thought.
But the ant can move the mountain –
I would want it to for me.

1 August 1989

Slave To Streak'd Skies

It is my lot and labor
To rivet my eyes upon
There where the others have
But vacant, fleeting looks.
It can't escape me,
The still remote storm
By high thin clouds
In the smiling sky foretold.
Nor the first, shy, unseen,
Stealthily falling snowflake of winter.
Weather-nature is to me
The innermost mirror of the soul,
The only true
And most reassuring one.
Raindrops are my real tears,
For which at ev'ry rainfall
I feel so sad and lon'some.
And even by the sunshine,
When they all brighten and sing,
My eyes can but behold
The streak'd skies I love so much,
Streak'd with few a cirrus
Fray'd to ice needles in the wind,
Now stretching and now writhing
Like my shapeless, unfail'd hopes.

29 August 1989

My Sweet Threshold Upon

Eyelids trembling
Like the last leaves on the trees
Likely to fall in the autumn wind;
Pieces of thought
Melting away like snowflakes
Pierced by sunbeams through:
I want to hold on,
Draw the suspense out,
Direct at pleasure
This fantastic play
Upon the sweet threshold of nought.
But the dark is waiting,
Ready to clutch my glistening scenery,
To catch the inexorable instant
Of the last conscious sigh of mine;
And to sink my guileless purpose
Into my pillow's silence.
And thereupon again
I shall have to face it –
That interminable tunnel
Of the already seen and heard,
Smelt and touch'd,
Of the already mockingly liv'd.
Without reins to steer the beast,
Without wings to fly;
Compell'd to act
Crazy, heart-burdensome intrigues
Upon the oneiric stage of mine.
Without suspended slumber magic,
Unable to unchain
The golden dreams of despair.
Until at the end of the tunnel –

If there be a new day to come –
The light, cold yet blinding,
Of the awak'ning
It dissolves my numbness.
Then I find myself breathing
In my friendly bed,
Left but with the vague shadows
Of elusory nocturnal visions.
With no more fears,
Nor cheerless moods to defeat;
Still, it's not the time at all
For fancy to fly!
If the threshold
Between awake and asleep
Is delicious and long,
Neverth'less the one
Between asleep and awake
Is flavorless and brief:
It tastes neither bitter nor sweet –
It tastes but real.

3–6 September 1989

The Hill

Still,
I see the watching hill
Bemoaning my will,
Causing me deep chill.

The little hill
From foot to top still
It makes me thrill
Down in the vill.

The hill, the hill, the hill,
It'll cause me to cry my fill
Till I stick up my black bill
On the sacred walls on the hill.

7 September 1989

A Ladder To Be Floored

You've put the moon
High in the sky,
My eyes led soon
To silently cry;

You've painted green
What was but black,
But never seen
My colored track;

You like the stone
That's hard and cold,
So you're alone
In your sweet hold.

The moon will rise
Above my head,
Till lovely lies
Sustain my thread;

The green will stain
Beneath the sun,
Till my loved pain
Turns into fun;

The clock is still
Upon my hours,
It brings me chill
And my life sours.

I see you smile
Behind sorrow,
Yet you beguile
Deep your tomorrow;

I see you there
Firm on the top,
And from up there
You make me stop;

You hear my sighs
As you turn away,
Still hips and thighs
Show me the way.

To love to live
Or to live to love,
I'm left but to leave
Since you're above;

The stone is wet
But it's too late,
Your eyes are set
Upon my fate;

See the ladder
I can but floor,
I feel sadder
Than ever the poor.

7 September 1989

Petrified

However much you shout
Nobody will hear you,
And the screech
Of your shattered hopes
Will die away inside
Your stony bosom.
Yea – to stone it's turned
Your ungoverned, unhappy joy!
Stone – heavy and motionless,
Shapeless, lifeless –
An unmeaning fossil
Lying on your heart.
It throbbed though,
And breathed – it lit up
With every little light
Reflected in every little thing;
It carried by itself
The clouds, changeful and passing,
The multifarious flight of birds,
The biting breeze of the evening,
The sigh for the longed-for rest
Near the end of the day,
And all what is worth
But for the fact of being able
To get the good of it.
Yet all is silence now:
No throbs, no thoughts,
Only the smooth wearing of time
Over a stone – cold and alone –
Which nothing can graze.

All is drearier
Than a flower's throes of death,
Than a poor wretch's bare booth.
All, all
Is unchanging stone,
Without even a shadow anymore
Of the slightest movement.
Neither laugh, nor cry.
Only regret.

17–18 September 1989

Colors And Sounds

I've been never ask'd
Just which is the color
I'd give to gladsom'ness,
Nor which one to wretchedness,
Lest my answer
Should be only one for both!
Well then to the former
I give some sable-green,
Because in black
My happiest days are cloth'd,
As well as in the emerald
Of unshatter'd hopes;
And to the latter
A bright vermilion,
The color itself
Of the plentiful blood
Spouting from undress'd cuts.
Yet – rather than colors –
It is sounds
That I love to pair with moods:
Joy is
The shrill whistle of a train
Which increases from afar,
Runs stunning and high
And dies posthaste away!
Sorrow is
The low sound of an organ,
Some dull pulsation
Ever-present though faint,
Which grows deafening

As soon as the mind's ears
Divert themselves from outer noises
To listen to
The silence inside.

29 September 1989

Why?

Why not let ourselves be carried
Toward shores unexplored,
Where the tide
It runs upstream,
Up to the river source?
Yonder eyes,
Though sunward turned,
They can discern the glows
Of heaven's most remote chasms;
Ears can hear,
In spite of all murmuring surfs,
The feeblest, inmost whispers on earth.
And a seagull
Flying overhead,
It will rouse our notice
More than every wonder,
Whereas the streams' anomaly
Will leave us unconcerned
As would a pebble
On the edge of a country road.
Still the singularity
Of such places themselves
Will render us suspicious and fearful,
As with unwonted awe pervaded.
We will thence struggle
Against the dread of seeing undone
Our lonesomeness' travail!
Yet no menace
Hangs over the shores,
Nor any typhoons over the horizon.

Why then let ourselves be carried
Toward such shores unexplored,
If we are thereat invaded
By the fear of probing them
Sooner than by our desire
To be carried back?

30 September–2 October 1989

Blamed In A Dream

Like sweet Emily –
Who while dreaming
Comes and upbraids
Me with my weakness,
Save then fondling
My slovenly soul –
I too follow
The dictates of my heart,
When, unable to take
My power in my hand –
And you succeeded
In taking yours, O Emily,
Even tho' after that
You'd miss your mark –
I grasp the sword
Of shiny steel
As smooth as looking-glass,
Beholding it,
Watching my scare
Reflected in the blade.
But it's worth nothing –
You would say, O Emily –
To wield the sword
So as to feel a false elation!
At least you dared!
And even tho' you came off beaten,
You may well appear to me
And blame my cowardice.

4 October 1989

All Things Are Messages

All things are messages
The eyes should be able to look into.
Messages without senders
Whose addressees are all of us,
Objects useful or useless
Anyway goad for the mind.
There can't be any things
Wholly beyond our depth
If we truly try to discover
The simplest message in them!
Real intelligence is a rare gift,
Uncommon is common sense!
What we seek above everything
Could lie just under our nose,
But if we can't read the thing
It won't ever be much too close.

4 October 1989

The Vacuum

The vacuum is ev'rywhere,
Where most things have to be seen
And where least it's believ'd to be.
In the lifeless bleakness
Within a richly furnish'd hall
As well as in the inextricableness,
Fascinating though insane,
Of the mind loose from reality.

The vacuum is
Want of inspiration,
Disjointed images and words
Which vainly run after a dream;
It is volition chaos,
A volcano of body's desires,
The slow and aglow flow of which
Slides down the spirit's mazes.

The vacuum is
Want of love,
Some chilly boulder
Weighing heart's bounty down;
It is desolation of the soul,
Left alone to fret
By the misery of the body,
Chain'd to the stillness of the night.

The vacuum is
Want of faith,
The fool's absurd and haughty
Conviction of omnipotence;
It is the harvest of sacrifices
To idols of marble and gold,
A somber procession in time
After winking fetishes.

The vacuum is
Want of courage,
The useless repress'd rage
Of an untam'd rebel temper;
It is intention tempest
With neither wind nor rain,
Some cowardly hurricane
Which dissolves in dead calm.

The vacuum is ev'rywhere,
In the majesty of sceneries
Seen by eyes unable to view,
And in the solemnity of tunes
Heard by ears unable to hearken.
It's where man labors most
And where least he deems himself alone.
The vacuum is the cognizance of the human state.

6 October 1989

I Saw Upon Faces

I saw upon faces
Yellowed with age
The ancient gaiety
Like dew trickle
From deep eyes down
Cheeks lean and drawn.
I saw in the sky
The aerial ballet
Of a few swallows,
Nearly a refrain
Calling for help,
Addressed to the past.
I heard from the poplars
Subdued whisperings
In the autumn wind –
Once loved rustle,
Now only the vain warning
Of disenchanted onlookers.
So the sentinels of dawn,
Which day after day
Silent wait but for sunset,
From beyond the mist
Of the weary horizon,
They keep watching
The old man make his way
With the heart viced
In the stranger evening,
While the stick
Creaks on the road,
Unmindful of his bourne.

7 October 1989

I Do Love Ye

I do love ye,
Woman I don't know
And though without ardor
I desire to meet.
I do love ye,
Splendid woman soulless
In azure attire dress'd,
Ochre-eyed and light brown-hair'd,
With skin smooth and complexion fair
Which line the heart of me.
Thrifty of your voice and smile,
Secretly keen on kindnesses
And on my turning over,
Jealous of nothing
But the unknown side of ye.
I do love ye,
In chaste fancies imprison'd,
No longer prey to terror,
Nor to passion.
Should you ever exist out of me.

12 October 1989

108

Distant Fanfares

Undistinguished clangors
Conveyed by the wind,
In background located,
Like an alarm bell
In a hidden corner sounded,
To warn of a danger
As unknown as real.
Our all-twisting manhood
Longing for misfortunes,
In the thoughtless warmth
Of the unwitting wish of dread,
Often cannot recognize
Carried in the air
The echoes and calls
Of distant fanfares:
Trumpets and drums
Festively played,
Coming from faraway hamlets.
First of all
The one, made smaller
And weighed down,
Of our inner spirit of serenity,
Drowned in the metropolis
Of everyday distress.

12 October 1989

Journey To The Peep Of The Day

Adamantine blinks
Shining through the amethyst
And ruby-adorned sky:
The child is treading
By the fireball blinded,
And drawn by the colors
Scattered all around.

Strips thinning,
Dying on the horizon,
At hand yet unreachable:
The boy is running
Under Prussian blue,
As excited and reckless
Onto untraced paths.

Numbers of fixed sparks
Making the boundless cloak
Visible and kind:
The man is hastening
Under unseen pictures
While the coil is unrolling
Toward the last turn.

Stalks of light
Piercing through the sky
Gilded to the depths:
The old man stops,
As scared of descrying
The sphere beyond the glow,
And of missing the final step.

17 October 1989

Waiting For The Ultimate Bound

Caught in trips through fragmented scenes
I evoke the champions of abandon.
They ride about immaterial lands
Searching for the key to freedom,
But they're slaves to my wait.
They ride, and search, and fight
Against the shortening night,
Silently aware of my round
Waiting for the ultimate bound.

23 October 1989

The Last Way Left

When the last shake
Has tailed away
Behind the corner of time
And no other beam
Runs through us from gloominess,
The mute words – indelible – are
The last way left to keep
The ungrown bud alive and
To make our hearts be not seized
By giggling melancholy – nearly
A want of vital dole –
Nor with the panic of Lethe.

31 October 1989

Leaves

A sound,
Some falling sigh
From the boughs of the trees;

Around
The stones we're nigh,
Like cold, bewildered bees.

The host,
In that strange tune
And the hearts on their travel;

We're lost
Like the leaves strewn
On the graveyard gravel.

5–6 November 1989

A Dawn Like Any Other Dawn

A new dawn
Illumines the ancient marbles
Laden with forgotten splendors
And abhorred heritages.
A little cloud
Is tinged with pink,
Pierced by the soft sun
Still hidden below the skyline,
Free from the baleful shadows.
Like a swan spreading its wings
The cloud extends,
Bringing its blithe whiteness
Beyond there where the sight
Had never reached before –
Beyond the memory of men.
Like flights parted
In a distant winter
And joined again nevermore,
Exuberant crowds migrate in silent
Excitement as the new day breaches.
A cry, liberating and joyous,
Insinuates itself into the cracks in the wall.
A dawn like any other dawn
Of a timid fall.
The same sun, the same sky, the same
Biting air of the morning – one only side.
One only spirit, one only yearning.
The shadow of the blame – birth
Of the unremembered monster –
Fades at the foot of the wall.

16 November 1989

The Sowing Place

Let me alight, O gentle
Mother Prime, on the sweet bottom
Of the coveted dale,
Girt with smooth slants and
Keeper of pleasant groves.
Let me drink
From its palpitating well,
Hidden in the deep of the forest,
Wherein the sun cannot make
Its rays arrive,
But only a mild lukewarmness.
Let me be inebriated
By its secret melodies,
That I may thereby
Be bound and carri'd
To the unseen skies of pleasure.
May I not have any fear
Of the shaggy passages to the vale,
Of its mysteries
And natural defenses,
For here drives me my restless
Soul. For here my body yearns,
Exhausted, in need of sleep.
In the most joyful shade,
In the most delightful wave
A man's mind can imagine,
Where the world is nothing but a nook,
Hours don't mark their passing,
Sorrow is let go by,
Love at last is the sower.

17 November 1989

115

Bahamas

The final touch
To a many-yeared enchanted flight.
Anew there I am – suspended and breathless.
I find myself enraptured
By black sparkling eyes,
Soothed by a blithe warming voice.
A gold-brown silhouette – such a
Bitter-sweet tantalizing cradle –
Forever entangled in my mind.
And – some well known whisper
Turned into stone – my bosom wanders
About the colorful ocean,
Looking for rest to come.
There beyond the olden deep – never
Fading away – a Bahamian dream of love.
Nowhere around the world – gentle pining
Memory – she runs away, far away.
Remembrance kills, to live retrieves.
Somewhere – she is.

22 August 1993

Back To The Cradle Gaol

The Search

There is a mirror/you never face
It's out of time/and out of space

You could behold /all things inside
And win the fear/bred by your pride

But yet the search/takes up your mind
That you disregard/all that you find

The way is winding/and full of snares
You may be true/but no one cares

There are people/who lead the game
Meanwhile they hide/the main real aim

And then you well/can say – I turn –
None is found and/still you must learn

Till you realize/the search is useless
And all have played/upon your goodness

At last you stop/and look for a sign
But none is left/to show you the line

So in the mirror/you'll see your breast
And him who said/there is no quest

The search will end/where it had begun
Where there was love/and care and fun.

4–5 March 1995

119

A Chased Uncanny Ship

Proudly ploughin' the belov'd wrappin' sea
And skillfully complyin' with the whistlin' crests,
Fearless on the move, the freedom ship is set
Against the threatenin' changeful sky.
She's chased, but she'll never run aground.
The sailor plays with the friendly breezes,
Unmindful of the docile steering wheel,
Whilst the mainsails shriek due to such a fury
As no man has ever seen in the stormwind.
She's urged, but she'll never get into calms.
Wander – wander round and round undaunted
Along the drowsin' waves of roarin' dreams
Until the circle unfolds through vertical clouds
And upon the summit of the vigilant mainyard
The lone crow changes into a flock of mews.
Someplace – far overseas – there beyond
The deep of the mind, the ship is awaited
By some coveted appeasin' mooring, where
The sailor's thirst will be quenched –
All sails shall be quietly unfurl'd in the sun.

3 April 1995

The Mind Of The Night

Hither and thither around my head
Starts and stays on the finest thread

Never close enough or even too much
Upon my breath the sweetest touch

A sinuous dance of fear and love
Throughout my soul – below and above

The stranger gaze into my eyes
Some inquirer of truth and lies

All over my body a thrill of pleasure
And deep inside a buried treasure

In want of laugh – in want of cry
This endless night without a sky

Slave to yesterday and tomorrow
A lone spirit in a well of sorrow

Clear but faint as a lovers' sigh
Sadness and joy so far so nigh.

20–21 April 1995

The Dragon

There! The Dragon flutters
Ejecting tongues of fire.
Here it is – so true, so near –
The old roaring beast
Which can't be killed.
Tho' much fed long since
It is not sated with me.
Its burning coils wrap me
Inhaling my breath
And tearing my flesh.
All ablaze inside,
All dark outside;
The day is like the night
Being the flame too bright.
Unrestingly its jaws
Will blow red fire,
Its merciless clutches
Will grip my limbs.
The inhuman fight will last
Until I am the one who wins,
Or until of my soul
But the sighs remain.
Of me,
Nothing but the bones.

24–25 July 1995

Ursa Major

I once heard of a starnaut
Who threw his ship thro' the stars,
Seeking the end of the universe
And the meaning of everything.
He was a lone space traveler
With but his thoughts as mates,
His mind as supreme driver
And never failing spur,
In endless search of secrets
Among planets and cosmic dust.
He cross'd throughout the Galaxy
And was amazed and frighten'd
Each time new worlds were reached.
He landed on stranger bodies,
On spheres of ice and liquid metal,
Through the arms and core of the Milky Way,
Where time seems not to elapse.
He saw what's veiled to any other man,
Not finding yet the Truth and The One,
Until he was close to forgetting
The place he'd left from long before.
Then tired, aware of the near end,
He finally found peace and rest
Around a well-known zone of heaven,
And discovered his primitive soul.
The powerful engine was still forever,
The ship stopped there forever.
You can look at it on high
Shining bright by Ursa Major
As its newborn eighth star.

26–27 July 1995

123

I (The Endless Trip)

I go, I go – everywhere I go –
And wherever I go – there I
Still have to go.
The moon follows
After my shade – it never
Lights up my step.
Landscapes change and
Solid stones crumble into
Grains of sand blown away.
I try to keep my own range
While all things change
And nobody cares
Wherefore my heart fares.
I just can't see that
My trip is a circle
Closed on itself.
I go, I go – always I go –
I'm like a guideless
Locomotive, whose steam
Never runs over.

2 August 1995

Restlessly

Start the fight
Feed the fire
Deep by night
Upon the wire.

The cut is deep
It makes me cry
I cannot leap
Nor make it dry.

The way is long
Up to the light
I'm not that strong
So as to be right.

I'd want to hush
To stop and stay
But I must rush
Onto my way.

9–16 August 1995

Silvia

From above the highest cloud
The eagle flew down
In large dizzy spirals,
Down to graze the desert,
And alighted in the shade
Of your gentle mind.
It captured your eye
And since then your soul
Was ravished forever.
These Indian tales are for you,
The sole white squaw I know,
And the only one
Able to enlarge my sight
And soothe my distress.
Do you really think
That you were born
In the wrong place?
Don't be unquiet,
Nor scared of yourself!
Free and pure spirits
Haven't got a home.
None, never, nowhere.
And you are one of them.
Unmistakably you are.

21 August 1995

How?

Your lips sign
The boundary that divides
Between always and never.

Your face encircles
All that I've not found
In the crazy runs of the past.

Your body sings
All those charming tunes
I've always wanted to hear.

How could I have not loved you?
How could I not love you?
How will I love you?

Your eyes enter
Deep into the soul of me,
And inside there have built my gaol.

25 August 1995

The World

The world.
Nothing save me
Nothing save me
Nothing save me.
I traced
My own destiny
And I was shown
All of it.
The world.
Nothing save me
Nothing save me
Nothing save me.
The world:
Life and everything,
Nobody,
But you.

26 August 1995

Burn

Burn, burn, burn
Sky and earth –
Fall all stars,
And dusky arms
Will slay the day.
Burn, burn, burn
The world
And all inside –
A demon laughs
As angels die.
Burn the air
With azure flames
Until of men
A mere squeal remains.
Burn all loves,
Remembrance stays –
Burn the past
And the future escapes.
All is thrown
In the burning gale,
While oblivion claims
Its final veil.
I'm in the middle
Of such disaster,
But my foul mind
Still runs to you
Though the speed
I throw myself
Can never be as high
As the burning whole's.

27 August 1995

129

Remember

Remember,
Treasures are the more precious
The more they're undiscovered
And the longer have been buried
In the depths of the soul.
So don't you lie to yourself,
Saying that you disregard
Any treasure once found,
Because you're cool and cruel,
Because you don't care
And don't lack anything!
Your eyes themselves talk
When your lips are still,
And well I feel from afar
When you weep, after playing,
Alone in the darkness.
What you've done
Nobody can do
Without the heart of you.
Love is blindness
And all I'd lost
Before you came
And drew it out
From my shelter of ice.
However it goes,
To joy or to sorrow,
All that is rescued
Well is worth seeing you,
Nothing doing but crying,
Being killed with your smile
And even letting you go
Your way to happiness.

Love will follow
Like a silent shade
And shall nevermore fade.
All this, remember.

27–28 August 1995

A Flower

You say you're used
To climbing on hills,
Searching for solitude
And wisdom, but did you ever
Climb on the mountain
Which cannot be seen
Until you get to its top?
Plenty of efforts
And resolute patience,
Sacrifice and standing pain
Are needed for it
Rather than knowledge.
But if you succeed
Without turning back
To see what is left behind
And if someone goes
After your shoulders,
If you really don't care
For what is under your feet
And you're not afraid
Of what you could find
Or of what you could lose,
Then you'll reach the summit,
Where – unpicked a flower –
You'll stand touching heaven.

29 August 1995

Quakes Down All The Planet!

Quakes down all the planet!
Echoes shouting loud and far
To wake our terror anew.
Huge clouds gathering up
Into black storms foretell
That what is coming is hell!

The bell gives a toll,
The last one to be heard
Before the earth falls
And turns to dead stone.
We've been calling disgrace,
Is this the doom of the human race?

Since the world was done
We've been looking for power,
We've grown rich through wars
And forgotten whence we come.
Are we now really going to disperse?
We the only castaways of the universe?

30 August 1995

Woken Is The Night

Woken is the night,
Still sealed and waiting
Behind the curtains –
The cup of gold is ready,
Filled with sweet poison
That but the dark lady
Can make me drink
With a smile on her lips.
The bed is well done,
And the clock is still
While the candle flickers
By exhausted whispers.
I look at the door
Which remains ajar –
Heartbeats run faster
But nobody shows through.

14 September 1995

If There Be

Broken I lie,
To shed tears upon this rock –
Upon this bed of cold stone
Which is the life of me.
The hurricane has come
And caught me naked
And asleep, it has
Crashed and raised me up,
To make me stand out
Like refulgent crystal.
But the thunders have gone
As quick as they'd come,
Leaving me to weep
Upon this ancient rock –
Still and flat anew,
To wait for the ultimate
Lethal lightning to come.
If there be any burst again.

3 October 1995

Glory's End

The painless warriors
And the loveless knights!
They do come unto me
With their icy lances
Aimed by their burning gazes.
They do come and make me stand up,
They do come and lift the stone
Which is weighing my heart down.
They do transfix the shield of sleep
And pierce through my bosom deep.
For Avalon does not exist
But in our dreaming minds,
For Lancelot stopped loving,
Merlin stopped mystifying
And Perceval stopped seeking
When we were still unborn.
For stains and shades by now
Cover each of us.
Nothing is worth
This epic labor.

9–10 October 1995

Tumble

Strange but plain is your desire
Right when I am falling down,
Falling straight into the fire;
Sturdy is your way to be
When you feel just like a bird
Whose wings could take it away,
But that cannot sing unheard.
So the pages of life will turn
Through clear and obscure days,
You don't know which ones to save
As your heart now goes, now stays.
A tumble is my whole life
Every time you see me cry;
And some page remains unturned
Lest your wings should no more fly.

30 October 1995

In Your Place

There must be a place
Where I can plunge my face
Which be neither my lean hands
Nor your throbbing breast;
There must be one somewhere
Near some sprouting flower
Which be no well of sorrow
But a cradle for our smiles.
Doings there would turn slow,
And our lives would sweetly flow
Without heat burning your desire
Nor clouds darkening my stare.
Should the wind not come
You shall blow my soul instead,
Should the sun not shine
You shall dry my eyes instead.
There then – as invisible wires
Binding us in one tight knot –
Tunes will breathe between us,
Seal my lips and loose your bosom;
Until you see beyond the barrier
What was hidden yet open wide
And know a tear is never as bitter
As to have to be too soon dried.

10–15 January 1996

Don't Cry Baby

Don't cry baby,
Don't spoil your smile.
Don't cry baby
Because you're lonely,
But leave your tears
In the cranny of your desire
And turn your worries off.
When you're alone
And I'm so far away,
If raindrops start falling
Take your friendly horn
And begin to play
The music you love.
Play happy tunes
And keep on rain or shine.
Play for me your life
Incessantly,
Play my voiceless line.

19–20 January 1996

Visions

Visions,
Fancies,
Dreamscapes.
Pink and blue
Shocking.
All mix
In a swarm
That whirls
In your brain.
But always,
All of a sudden,
A new day
Is born.
And all that
Remains
Is the reality
You make.
Then look!
Your life
Is unfolding.

21 January 1996

Living Blue

Tired eye,
As wet and consumed
As a pebble
Standing still
Under rainfalls,
You keep on
Following
The rosy cloud
That wanders
Across the sky.
Like a child
Abandoned alone
You want to seek
A place of peace,
Of love and warmth,
But the cloud
Disappears
Like dispelled vapor
At each sundown –
When the blue cloak
Turns into black –
To appear smaller
At each new dawn.
And you keep
On following,
You keep on hunting,
On wanting, on wanting,
Though the sight
Runs shorter,
The breath
Runs weaker,

The beat
Runs slower.
Your stare
Dives higher
In your living blue,
After the cloud
That flies
Farther every night.
She turns
Round and round
Until you seem
To catch her,
But she always
Escapes before
You can touch her.
Then she flies
Free and untamed,
She flies away
Carried along
In a dreaming breeze,
Up to the edge
Of your living blue.
Until no color
Can be seen anymore
And the cloud
Vanishes in a tiny
Point of light
Falling down
Beyond the horizon.
But you – tired eye –
Want to keep
On watching,
Want to keep
On following,
On wanting, on wanting.
You can't see that
The sky is empty,

The night is naked,
Your tears have dried.
All is staining
Within your silence
As you get lost –
Moveless –
In your living blue.

6 February 1996

Against The Night

Shadows run crazy
Through golden thoughts
But the nought
Can't fill the passing hole.

Cloths of lead
And shoes of earth
Push my shouting body
Out from here.

Smoke and dust
Like stone air
Cover crystal sighs
That break against the night.

7 February 1996

By The Bonfire

The night has flown
Above the crackles of the flames,
Above us shouting by the bonfire:
Yellow tonguing on high
And violet below,
Red deep inside our embers.
There were loose bodies
And vagabond minds,
All slaves to bourneless souls.
I've felt the more alone
The more people
Were dancing 'round the fire.
And the night has fallen
Raw over the flames
And over us shouting.
The silence has come
Crawling into us
And flying higher
Than the crazy sparks
Flashing from the fire.
Somebody wanted to nurse
Some blue dream by the bonfire,
But joy is burned in the blaze
As sorrow comes out inviolate.

31 October 1996

Hidden Message

In the end
Let it come to me
Or let it slip away,
Vain is my obduracy.
Echoes thunder loud taking
Yells from inside
Over your warming breath.
Up and down,
Sighs and tears
In your scared eyes
Leave me defenseless,
Void and swinging.
In the mirror
Answers face both of us.

4 November 1996

Common Man

Raise your
Wandering head
High above
Your hermit heart –
Wonders will no longer
Escape the dreams of you.
Greedily embrace
My laughing sorrow
Within your dumb
Crystal-sigh-fill'd breast,
As in a bitter-sweet
Melody ballet.
Kiss my hair
Against the horizon,
So that you
Can't see me but
As an edgeless
Fading shadow.
There I will stand,
Mute and screaming
At the same time –
No more thief
Of weeping kisses,
No more one night hero,
No more tear drawer,
No more any lover –
Naked fallen
Upon your shining life.
Then you'll see me
Go back where
I had issued from.

Then you'll see me
As a common man.

13–14 November 1998

Alone

See the comet
Divide the sky in two.
One is happy
And one is sad,
Yet I do not fly
Through either,
For there's no good and bad.
The comet's gone
But it will return;
I'm far alone,
Far alone on the line,
Far alone from mine.
The skies reunite
And I'm in between;
I'm still alone,
Far alone and unseen.
The skies are one
Before my eyes;
I'm still alone,
Far alone and gone.
Can you reach that far
To my lone star?
Say yes or no,
Anyway I go.
Say yes or no,
Still the comet
Will be back
And go once more.
Yes or no
Alone I go.

19 November 1998

Back To The Cradle Gaol

To succeed or to fail,
When there's nothing left to bet
All you can do is just get
Back to the cradle gaol.

26 August 1999

Glastonbury

I have dampened
The parched lips of mine
By avidly mouthing
The plumbeous brume
Which eternal ensconces
The remnants of myth.

Treading on the soil
Incorporeally real,
And sodden with yells
From epigones of dream,
I have made all
My useless attempts
To purloin the love,
The odium, the ire,
The undefeated might
Of reposing heroes.

But all that my body
Could abstract from there
Is shatters of mould,
Abased and tarnished,
Dissolving in the exhaling
Struggles of fame.

As in a desperate quest
Anew proclaimed, I have
Made those meads
My own battleground,
So as to draw vigor
From hills and tors
And have my courage renewed.

But deeds of giants
Yonder wait, sleeping
On the bottom of the
Immovable blanket
Of primeval mist,
For the sun to tear aside
The veil of time once more,
While my step has been
Leading me waywardly
From one to another
Secret abode of the dale.

Wars and invasions
Of yore are swallowed
By ages, nevertheless
Still the profaned
Spirit of the Britons
Restlessly quivers among
The vaults unrecalled.

With them I have
Wandered through vast,
Silenced moors,
In search of the evidence
For the wait to be ceased
For good for evermore.

But as totally in vain
I have pursued there
The druidical force
Evanesced in me, so
The unavertable rise
Of a king long announced
Is yet far to come.

9 September 1999

Retrospective

Against my silly lament
You screamed out your innocence,
Before my pointless strength
You exhibited your impotence.
But yet your tears
Could neither wet my hands
Nor stem their tireless tremor.
Eke your admonition
Could never soothe my boldness
Nor turn it to apter objective.
And so my stalwart onset
Has died down, slowly slain,
Similar to flame devouring the air –
Until of the air no traces remain.

10 September 1999

Bliss

Bliss is a kiss
Sealing your mouth,
Stifling not your breath.
It is a word
Enlightening your thought,
Clipping not your wish.
It is the sound
Of your loose soul
That like spurting gushes
Bursts from unsuspected cleft.
Don't let it fly away
Before having seized its secret.
Bliss is a minute
Impressed as indelible slur
On the epidermis of your life.

10 September 1999

Accidental Verse

Dedi

Wiser would you have been
Had you never stolen
The richest sighs from me,
Together with my only treasure.
Aphonic silhouettes
Sneaking hang about
As perfect shapes
That hardly throw any shadows.
Inscrutable, your glance
Does plunge its blade
Deep into my innuendo.
Liquid figures
Redescend my body
Down to my toes,
As your eyes and smile
Do remain attached
To my composed façade.
Still my pupils
Have you reside
In my witless head
And evermore my words
Fail to lay hold on you.

12 September 1999

The Wind To A Violet

The wind did thunder
To a weeny violet:
'You'd better make haste
And find out shelter –
How can you not dread
The coming tempest?
I'm but the herald
Of the brewing fury –
How could you stand
Its fiercest raging?
For one gust of mine
Would pull up too easily
That feeble stem of yours –
Why don't you hurry then
To look for a safer den?'
So bent in the blast,
But yet calm and fast
The floweret riposted:
'This is my own place
And I would never move –
I shall endure the strife
For that is my life.
What may elements fear
With their immense power?
I can't run from here
And I'm but a flower.'

13 September 1999

Stars

'Hey you dimmed – mine sisters brilliant,
We are not to be spent on effulgence – never!
For all should we keep on burning – you know,
But as glimmers would we be descried though.
And no distance indeed is our shroud,
But of unaware men the tumult too loud.
Even so we are to flare in eons uncounted
Such being our thankless necessary effort –
Why then would we care for them unmindful,
Them who but whisper beneath our twinkle?
Ever-blazing forges we were born distant giants
So as to cradle time and the world turn around –
Let them believe themselves undisputed rulers
Of what we disguisedly do command and bound.'

14 September 1999

Beethoven And The Balm-Cricket

Treading ponderously in the mum eventide
In the thick of a coppice of shrubs and bushes
The Genius by name bygone in ethereal disguise
Turned out to fall upon a balm-cricket chirping.

BALM-CRICKET

'Who art thou?
Do I know thee?
Thou resemblest a shade,
But whose ever ghost?'

BEETHOVEN

'I was creator
Before man created,
As spectre I wander –
A hostage of time.
Dost thou grasp me though,
Insect humdrum but smart?
One day then did come
I could no more hear,
Thenceforth music itself
Did well from mine hands.
How canst thou fathom
A symphony of wonders
Just unsensed by men?
Thou who keepest uttering
But one twosome of notes?'

BALM-CRICKET

'I am no musician
And I do not presume,
Yet so far I do apprehend
Thy despondent misery,
If thou turnedst unto me –
Simple balm-cricket, not man –
And didst venture to explain
The whys of thine errant pain.'

15 September 1999

Nature And Mind

Once upon a timeless day it happened
That twain such titans as Nature and Mind
By chance ran at long last into each other.

NATURE

'So here it is the greater Mind,
The chief and crucial labor of mine!
Hence are you genuinely that one
To whom each entity is bound to bow?'

MIND

'Precisely I am the one you say
And there's nothing in the world I can't cover or weigh;
You fall within my field of survey as well
And had better wonder what at the beginning befell.'

NATURE

'I won't discuss your subtle apologies,
I only want you to answer one question barely:
Could you ever conceive or create such marvels,
As admirable and perfect themselves
As all the ones that can be viewed everywhere and pertain
To my boundless, uncontested domain?'

MIND

'Your reason – I see – has been misled in sooth,
Do thence remember this only truth:
It is definitely you that nurses these treasures,
But it is me alone that now rules and measures;
For it was no sooner than I was actually born
That you got out of your empty perfection
And attained completely your self-perception.'

17–18 September 1999

I Tried

I tried to stop the lightning in vain
Standing naked under pelting rain.
But one can never rest on heaven's cry,
For too grand a force it is hurled by.

18 September 1999

A Mirage Of Yours

Maybe you jeer
At my words
And deeds,
But won't you
Ever realize
What is told
And done
Is just that which
You thought
You would for aye shun?

18 September 1999

A Recurrence Of Mine

Reap my love
Before it goes dry,
No longer dare I
Keep it green on the sly.

18 September 1999

The Oak Tree And The Nightingale

'Why do you always come
Alighting hither and thither
And perturb the quietude of me?'
Said the secular oak tree
To the early nightingale.
After long lasted restraint there was more,
'With your intermittent chirrup
You fluster the pace else impassible
Of my mute, far-reaching hours.
Your wings were not spreading yet
That I lavished shade and coolness
On the underlying lawn by then.
Why do you persist all day
In bewildering so the abiding
Susurration of my companion wind
Through the rustled frondage of mine?
You do but confound my perception of ages
And irksomely tickle my limbs
With restless flutters near here
In the midst of my harassed leafage.'
'Puissant and majestic oak tree,'
Did answer then the birdie back,
'Does my singing upset truly
The seraphical safeness of yours,
Or does it by any chance shake,
Make your sturdy foundations quake?
I just could never toss at all
The sprigs and leaves from your trunk –
Do you really fear I can make
Your robust roots and boughs break?

Well you know how many wings
Have been vibrating 'mong your branches,
And how many more will come
Once mine has flown and gone.
You therefore are the potent oak tree –
Would you rid yourself at last
Of a harmless nightingale like me?
I could neither impair your time
Nor be the thief of your shadow,
But if you don't wish me
To come round here – nevermore –
Who will share with you
The joy for daybreak,
The cuddle of the wind,
The embrace of nightfall?
Who will ever share with you
The awareness of your solemn force?
Who will share with you
The burden of your moveless aging?
I last but few seasons,
Yet I can discover through you
The uncoverable vastness of time.
You always live one only scene,
But I am able and happy
To carry singing to you
The remote, stupendous variety
Of all fugitive murmurs from the earth.'

21 September 1999

Lady Strange (Has Come And Rocked My Cradle Gaol)

Whoever is this lady
Who calls herself but Dedi,
If not a shade again
Just slid into my den?

Too well I know my heart
Could swiftly fall apart,
Yet right because she's chill
I can't resist the thrill!

22 September 1999

Quantum Leap

Like a selfless particle – hereabout am I –
Don't you dare ask how come or why;
Doomed to vanish then to reappear,
Caprice of nature unstable and queer,
Forced by forces I cannot control
To jumps into being wanting in soul.
Crazy bouncing from whole to nought
Just to graze your senses and thought,
Unsubstantial entity – smart trick of who? –
Getting to nowhere though gotten by you;
Emerged out of chaos caught asleep,
Condemned to exist but as quantum leap.

30 September 1999

Adult Lullaby

Quick, quick, quick – tell your tricky trick,
Hop, hop, hop – get no whop in swap;
Ye, ye, ye – be no busy bee,
Toc, toc, toc – never shock the clock.

Ding, dong, dang – no more daylong pang,
C'mon, run, c'mon – fun is what you shun;
Rush, ssh, hush – flee from sunset's blush,
Dumb, sleep, numb – by love overcome.

On, on, on – don't keep holding on,
Sob, sob, sob – watching's a bad job;
Aye, aye, aye – near here may I stay,
Nay, nay, nay – till the close of day.

30 September 1999

Passions

The warm liquid entrails
Of wild relentless thinkings
Drip from the nostrils of inanimate guises,
Frigid porcelain faces only pervaded
With the vibrant frenzy of slackening passions.
Passions still alive and not yet curbed,
Dreading as much to fade away
As to be entrapped inside the body
Of fossil memories, squashed and flattened
Like veins of crystal rock,
Oppressed by layers of heart-effused
And chill-solidified magma.
Passions that urge the slow flow
Of the fine grains of the sandglass,
Crying their life and need of embodiment out,
Shouting hushward out of rest
Their desperate, sweeping bondage.
But masks dull and glowless
Are their sole passage through the dimness
Which like wrapping cloak
Chokes their waving blaze.
And inexorably meantime
Those thinkings trickle drop after drop,
So as to furrow those adamant visages,
Dampening that frenzy gradually,
Diluting those passions into the wastage
Of days deprived of all recollections.
They trickle low down
And are nonchalantly collected forever
Into the crucible of love's idle endeavor.

6 October 1999

Self-Reflections

Brotherhood – mates of dispelled wakes,
Yawning irrision at yourselves
Mirrored in my reluctant semblance,
Expose your cynical profiles
Through the amorphous glass
Of your full-blank wide screens!

Brotherhood – stock of silly sentries,
Wasting the power of yourselves
Away to inexistent raiders,
Show me your useless weapons
And lay bare your scare
Before my scanning eyes!

You who keep on coming after me –
Secret brothers from secret kinship –
Let your hiding selves be spotted,
That face to face I may finally ask:
'I am your self – I well can see,
But for my sake – who are you to me?'

7 October 1999

Letter From An Evicted Painter

Ochre iris hatched
In turquoise stolen from
A Caribbean wavelet, so
I love to remember you.
You peeled motes of infinite
Away, while getting
Lost – unseeing – in your
Whispered mulishness.
Time had stopped,
To gaze on you, as you
Let its blow dissolve
The colors from the palette,
Drawing from which – and
Tracing over the sketches
Of love – I was trying
To depict your life.

7 October 1999

The King Of The Fax

First burst forth His huge majestic belly
Popping like a regal flood of vibrant jelly;
Only later come His handcut tinplate crown,
Turning droll the bowl of His face into a frown.

His Royal Highness never wants to hold the scepter,
Still He is our Bunker Sovereign and supreme inceptor;
We made Him the Monarch of our village so lax
And simply called Him the King of the Fax.

His Majesty The King Popi I grants imprimatur in year 1999

8 October 1999

Printed in the United Kingdom
by Lightning Source UK Ltd.
9380700001B